ARKAL1

humble feelings

INSPIRATIONAL WISDOM FROM C.S. LEWIS, RICH MULLINS AND OTHERS

Andrew Kalitka

WINEPRESS WP PUBLISHING

Packaged by WinePress Publishing, PO Box 428, Enumclaw, WA 98022. The views expressed or implied in this work do not necessarily reflect those of WinePress Publishing. The author(s) is ultimately responsible for the design, content, and editorial accuracy of this work.

ISBN 1-57921-374-x
Library of Congress Catalog Card Number: 2001088417

*To anyone who is wholly searching for a
deeper understanding of God.*

Introduction

In *The Abolition of Man*, C.S. Lewis discusses an elementary school textbook from the 1940s in which a fallacy was introduced to children. This fallacy has multiplied in prominence since that time. In the textbook, a well known story about Samuel Taylor Coleridge at a waterfall was quoted. The story places two tourists at a waterfall where one calls it "sublime" and the other calls it "pretty." Coleridge, aware of both remarks, agrees with the first judgment but strongly disagrees with the second. This is where the writers of the textbook interject with the comment that Lewis was concerned about. The writers say, "When the man said *That is sublime*, he appeared to be making a remark about the waterfall. . . . Actually . . . he was not making a remark about the waterfall, but a remark about his own feelings. What he was saying was really, *I have feelings associated in my mind with the word 'Sublime,'* or shortly, *I have sublime feelings*. This confusion is continually present in language as we use it. We appear to be saying something very important about something: and we are only saying something about our own feelings."

After quoting this from the textbook, Lewis goes on to thoroughly examine the dangerous ideas presented and their logical conclusions. At the time he was writing, Lewis' evaluation probably seemed to his contemporaries to be an unlikely prediction of the future of education. However, reading *The Abolition of Man* at the start of the 21st century is like reading a description of our current educational situation and a prescription for its cure. I am not going to summarize Lewis' entire book, but I would like to quote a statement Lewis makes early on: "The feelings which make a man call an object sublime are not sublime feelings but feelings of veneration. If *This is sublime* is to be reduced at all to a statement about the speaker's feelings, the proper translation would be *I have humble feelings*."

Lewis' point is that when someone takes a good look at something, the origin of his or her feelings about it comes from the object, not the observer. The object "makes the first move," so the speak, and our humble feelings receive signals being sent from the image in front of us. If our feelings are inconsistent with those that the object would normally evoke, then our feelings are not humble, and we'd might as well be looking at nothing at all. Our feelings must be humble in order for us to perceive reality.

So when I entitled this book *Humble Feelings,* I was mainly referring to what C.S. Lewis talks about in *The Abolition of Man.* But I think this idea can also be related to the general idea of humility and the major difference between how humility is viewed by the Judeo-Christian worldview and how it is viewed by the current postmodern worldview. From a postmodernist perspective, the most humble people are the ones who do not believe in absolute truth. If you think that every possible thought, feeling, and action is equally good, then according to postmodernism you are about as humble as a person can get. However, according to a Judeo-Christian worldview, the more a person submits his or her thoughts, feelings, and actions to the framework of absolute truth, the more humble the person is. In Numbers 12:3, the Bible says that Moses was "a very humble man, more humble than anyone else on the face of the earth." And guess what Moses had done—he received the Ten Commandments from God! From the worldview of postmodernism, Moses could have been called the most self-absorbed bigot alive. But according to the Bible, he was the most humble person.

In *Humble Feelings,* I have included many quotes from writers, poets, and songwriters past and present who understood and believed what the Judeo-Christian view of humility is when they said what they said. I hope that this book will help bring you to a better understanding of what it is like to view the world with a Judeo-Christian worldview.

Andrew Kalitka
Gloucester, Massachusetts

Promised Land
State Park,
Pennsylvania

I believe that what I believe is what makes me what I am.
I did not make it, no it is making me. It is the very truth of God
and not the invention of any man.

—*Rich Mullins*

If our religion is something objective, then we must never avert our eyes from those elements in it which seem puzzling or repellent; for it will be precisely the puzzling or the repellent which conceals what we do not yet know and need to know.

—C.S. Lewis

Flies
Voss, Norway

Lynn Canal,
Alaska

Promised Land
State Park,
Pennsylvania

Colorado Springs, Colorado

I know that many wiser and better Christians than I in these days do not like to mention Heaven and hell even in a pulpit. I know, too, that nearly all the references to this subject in the New Testament come from a single source. But then that source is Our Lord Himself. People will tell you it is St. Paul, but that is untrue. These overwhelming doctrines are dominical. They are not really removable from the teaching of Christ or of His Church. If we do not believe them, then our presence in this church is great tom-foolery. If we do, we must sometime overcome our spiritual prudery and mention them.

—C.S. Lewis

Skagway,
Alaska

The Church's one foundation is Jesus Christ her Lord;
She is His new creation by water and the Word:
From heaven He came and sought her to be His holy bride;
With His own blood He bought her, and for her life He died.

—Samuel J. Stone and Samuel S. Wesley

Gill,
Massachusetts

Colorado Springs,
Colorado

Ipswich,
Massachusetts

The infinite value of each human soul is not a Christian doctrine. God did not die
for man because of some value He perceived in him. The value of each human soul
considered simply in itself, out of relation to God, is zero. As St. Paul writes, to have
died for valuable men would have been not divine but merely heroic; but God died
for sinners. He loved us not because we were lovable, but because He is Love. It may
be that He loves all equally—He certainly loved all to the death—and I am not
certain what that expression means. If there is equality, it is in His love, not in us.

—C.S. Lewis

16

Mt. McKinley,
Alaska

When people object . . . that if Jesus was God as well as Man, then He had an unfair advantage which deprives Him for them of all value, it seems to me as if a man struggling in the water should refuse a rope thrown to him by another who had one foot on the bank, saying, "Oh but you had an unfair advantage." It is because of His advantage that He can help.

—C.S. Lewis

Redwood
National
Park,
California

Braham,
Minnesota

This is my Father's world,
and to my listening ears
All nature sings, and round me
rings the music of the spheres.
This is my Father's world!
I rest me in the thought
of rocks and trees,
of skies and seas—
His hand the wonders wrought.
—Maltbie D. Babcock and
Franklin L. Sheppard

Yukon River,
Yukon Territory,
Canada

Newbury,
Massachusetts

This is my Father's world—The birds their carols raise;
The morning light, the lily white, declare their Maker's praise.
This is my Father's world! He shines in all that's fair;
In the rustling grass I hear Him pass—He speaks to me everywhere.
—Maltbie D. Babcock and Franklin L. Sheppard

Redwood
National
Park,
California

Hawkins,
Texas

It was not for societies or states that Christ died, but for men. In that sense Christianity must seem to secular collectivists to involve an almost frantic assertion of individuality. But then it is not the individual as such who will share Christ's victory over death. We shall share the victory by being in the Victor. A rejection, or in Scripture's strong language, a crucifixion of the natural self is the passport to everlasting life. Nothing that has not died will be resurrected. That is just how Christianity cuts across the antithesis between individualism and collectivism.

—C. S. Lewis

Manchester,
Massachusetts

Holderness,
New Hampshire

Neither the individual nor the community as popular thought
understands them can inherit eternal life, neither the natural self,
nor the collective mass, but a new creature.
—C.S. Lewis

North Hero
State Park,
Vermont

Manchester,
Massachusetts

Denali
National
Park,
Alaska

There's more that rises in the morning than the sun,
more that shines in the night than just the moon.
There's more than just this fire here that keeps me warm
in a shelter that is larger than this room.
There's a loyalty that's deeper than mere sentiment,
a music higher than the songs that I can sing.
The stuff of earth competes for the allegiance
I owe only to the giver of all good things.
—*Rich Mullins and Steve Cudworth*

Lynn Canal,
Alaska

If I find in myself a desire which no experience in this world can satisfy,
the most probable explanation is that I was made for another world.
—C. S. Lewis

Near Juneau,
Alaska

Grand Canyon,
Arizona

Darlington
Provincial
Park,
Ontario,
Canada

I can imagine someone saying that he dislikes my idea of heaven as a place where we are patted on the back. But proud misunderstanding is behind that dislike. In the end that Face which is the delight or the terror of the universe must be turned upon each of us either with one expression or with the other, either conferring glory inexpressible or inflicting shame that can never be cured or disguised. I read in a periodical the other day that the fundamental thing is how we think of God. By God Himself, it is not! How God thinks of us is not only more important, but infinitely more important.

—C.S. Lewis

Niagara Falls,
Ontario,
Canada

At the worst, we know enough of the spiritual to know that we have fallen short of it, as if the picture knew enough of the three-dimensional world to be aware that it was flat.

—C.S. Lewis

Grand Canyon,
Arizona

Next to
Lynn Canal,
Alaska

Near Wrangell,
Alaska

A lightning flash, my pounding heart
A breaching whale, a shooting star
Give testimony that You are
And my soul wells up with hallejujahs.
—Chris Rice

Near Oku,
Cameroon,
Africa

When through the woods and forest glades I wander
And hear the birds sing sweetly in the trees,
When I look down from lofty mountain grandeur
And hear the brook and feel the gentle breeze
Then sings my soul, my Savior God, to Thee:
How great Thou art, how great Thou art!
Then sings my soul, my Savior God, to Thee:
How great Thou art, how great Thou art!

—Stuart K. Hine

North Hero
State Park,
Vermont

Sabga,
Cameroon,
Africa

Near Haines, Alaska

All our merely natural activities will be accepted, if they are offered to God, even the humblest, and all of them, even the noblest, will be sinful if they are not. Christianity does not simply replace our natural life and substitute a new one; it is rather a new organisation which exploits, to its own supernatural ends, these natural materials. No doubt, in a given situation, it demands the surrender of some, or of all, our merely human pursuits; it is better to be saved with one eye, than, having two, to be cast into Gehenna. But it does this, in a sense, *per accidens*—because, in those special circumstances, it has ceased to be possible to practise this or that activity to the glory of God.

—C.S. Lewis

Next to
Lynn Canal,
Alaska

He made the night
He made the day
Spread the earth upon the water
Made the heavens and the rain
Look at the sky, see its design
The very same creator is the one who gave us life.

—Rebecca St. James and Tedd T.

Clouds
Out
Airplane
Window

Newbury,
Massachusetts

Near Fairbanks,
Alaska

Never, in peace or war, commit your virtue or your happiness to the future.
Happy work is best done by the man who takes his long-term plans somewhat
lightly and works moment to moment "as to the Lord." It is only our *daily*
bread that we are encouraged to ask for. The present is the only time in which
any duty can be done or any grace received.

—C.S. Lewis

Tundra Plants

North of
Arctic Circle,
Alaska

Earth's crammed with heaven;
And every common bush afire with God;
But only he who sees, takes off his shoes,
The rest sit round it and pluck blackberries.
—*Elizabeth Barrett Browning*

Mfomakap,
Cameroon,
Africa

Iditarod Trail
Race
Headquarters,

Wasilla,
Alaska

All Thy works with joy
surround Thee,
Earth and heaven reflect
Thy rays,
Stars and angels sing
around Thee,
Center of unbroken praise.
Field and forest,
vale and mountain,
Flowery meadow,
flashing sea,
Chanting bird and
flowing fountain
Call us to rejoice in Thee.
—Henry Van Dyke

Promised Land
State Park,
Pennsylvania

Salmon
Swimming
Upstream

Near Wrangell,
Alaska

You who live in eternity
hear the prayers of those of us who live in time.
We can't see what's ahead
and we cannot get free from what we've left behind.
—*Rich Mullins*

Braham,
Minnesota

Denali
Mountains,
Alaska

Bar Harbor,
Maine

You remember the old puzzle as to whether the owl came from the egg or the egg
from the owl. The modern acquiescence in universal evolutionism is a kind of
optical illusion, produced by attending exclusively to the owl's emergence from the
egg. We are taught from childhood to notice how the perfect oak grows from the
acorn and to forget that the acorn itself was dropped by a perfect oak. We are
reminded constantly that the adult human being was an embryo, never that the life
of the embryo came from two adult human beings. We love to notice that the
express engine of today is the descendant of the "Rocket"; we do not equally
remember that the "Rocket" springs not from some even more rudimentary engine,
but from something much more perfect and complicated than itself—namely, a man
of genius. The obviousness or naturalness which most people seem to find in the
idea of emergent evolution thus seems to be a pure hallucination.

—C.S. Lewis

North Hero
State Park,
Vermont

What can be more foolish than to think that all this rare fabric
of heaven and earth could come by chance, when all the skill of
science is not able to make an oyster?

—*Jeremy Taylor*

Near Oku,
Cameroon,
Africa

Army Ants

Mfomakap,
Cameroon,
Africa

Oslo,
Norway

If you asked twenty good men today what they thought the highest of the virtues, nineteen of them would reply, Unselfishness. But if you had asked almost any of the great Christians of old, he would have replied, Love. You see what has happened? A negative term has been substituted for a positive, and this is of more than philological importance. The negative idea of Unselfishness carries with it the suggestion not primarily of securing good things for others, but of going without them ourselves, as if our abstinence and not their happiness was the important point. I do not think this is the Christian virtue of Love. The New Testament has lots to say about self-denial, but not about self-denial as an end in itself. We are told to deny ourselves and take up our crosses in order that we may follow Christ; and nearly every description of what we shall ultimately find if we do so contains an appeal to desire.

—C.S. Lewis

Oslo,
Norway

I suddenly remembered that no one can enter heaven except as a child; and nothing is so obvious in a child—not in a conceited child, but in a good child—as its great and undisguised pleasure in being praised. Not only in a child, either, but in a dog or a horse. Apparently what I had mistaken for humility had, all these years, prevented me from understanding what is in fact the humblest, the most childlike, the most creaturely of pleasures—nay, the specific pleasure of the inferior: the pleasure of a beast before men, a child before its father, a pupil before his teacher, a creature before its Creator.

—C. S. Lewis

Braham,
Minnesota

Caddo Lake
State Park,
Texas

Sabga,
Cameroon,
Africa

They (the world) said boy you just follow your heart
but my heart just led me into my chest.
They said follow your nose
but the direction changed every time I went and turned my head.
They said boy you just follow your dreams
but my dreams were only misty notions.
But the Father of hearts and the Maker of noses and the Giver of dreams
He's the one I've chosen and I will follow Him.

—*Rich Mullins and Beaker*

Sun Shining
Through
Lighthouse

North Truro,
Massachusetts

Then in time Jesus came to be for us
And His Coming made our life a song
And His Word is the chorus
Is the Light that is burning
Is the truth beyond learning
Is the reason we sing.

—Michael Card and Phil Naish

Eastham,
Massachusetts

Eastham,
Massachusetts

Deerfield,
New Hampshire

We do not want merely to *see* beauty, though, God knows, even that is bounty enough. We want something else which can hardly be put into words—to be united with the beauty we see, to pass into it, to receive it into ourselves, to bathe in it, to become part of it. . . . At present we are on the outside of the world, the wrong side of the door. We discern the freshness and purity of morning, but they do not make us fresh and pure. We cannot mingle with the splendours we see. But all the leaves of the New Testament are rustling with the rumour that it will not always be so. Some day, God willing, we shall get *in*. When human souls have become as perfect in voluntary obedience as the inanimate creation is in its lifeless obedience, then they will put on its glory, or rather that greater glory of which Nature is only the first sketch. For you must not think that I am putting forward any heathen fancy of being absorbed into Nature. Nature is mortal; we shall outlive her. When all the suns and nebulae have passed away, each one of you will still be alive. Nature is only the image, the symbol; but it is the symbol Scripture invites me to use. We are summoned to pass in through Nature, beyond her, into that splendour which she fitfully reflects.

—C. S. Lewis

Promised Land
State Park,
Pennsylvania

Holderness,
New Hampshire

Woolwich,
Maine

Well the grass will die
And the flowers fall
But Your Word's alive
And it will be after all.
And everywhere I go I see You.
—Rich Mullins

St. Croix
State Park,
Minnesota

Agama Lizard

Mfomakap,
Cameroon,
Africa

All creatures of our God and King,
Lift up your voice and with us sing,
Alleluia, Alleluia!
Thou burning sun with golden beam,
Thou silver moon with softer gleam,
O praise Him, O praise Him!
Alleluia, Alleluia! Alleluia!
—St. Francis of Assisi (translated by William H. Draper)

Next to
Lynn Canal,
Alaska

Thou rushing wind that art so strong,
Ye clouds that sail in heaven along,
O praise Him! Alleluia!
Thou rising morn in praise rejoice,
Ye lights of evening, find a voice:
O praise Him, O praise Him!
Alleluia, Alleluia! Alleluia!
—St. Francis of Assisi

Near Oku,
Cameroon,
Africa

And all ye men of tender heart,
Forgiving others, take your part,
O sing ye! Alleluia!
Ye who long pain and sorrow bear,
Praise God and on Him cast your care:
O praise Him, O praise Him!
Alleluia, Alleluia! Alleluia!
—St. Francis of Assisi

72

Oslo,
Norway

Let all things their Creator bless,
And worship Him in humbleness,
O praise Him! Alleluia!
Praise, praise the Father, praise the Son,
And praise the Spirit, Three in One:
O praise Him, O praise Him!
Alleluia, Alleluia! Alleluia!
—St. Francis of Assisi

Bibliography

Many C.S. Lewis quotes came from the following works:

Lewis, C.S. *The Abolition of Man* (New York: Simon & Schuster, 1996).

Lewis, C.S. *The Weight of Glory and Other Addresses* (New York: Simon & Schuster, 1996).

Songs

Page 8. "Creed" by Rich Mullins and Beaker, © 1993 BMG Songs, Inc. (ASCAP) and Kid Brothers of St. Frank Publishing (ASCAP), *A Liturgy, A Legacy, and a Ragamuffin Band* (Nashville: Reunion, 1993).

Page 14. "The Church's One Foundation" by Samuel J. Stone and Samuel S. Wesley, *Praise!* (Grand Rapids, Michigan: Zondervan, 1979).

Pages 20–21. "This is My Father's World" by Maltbie D. Babcock and Franklin L. Sheppard, *Praise!* (Grand Rapids, Michigan: Zondervan, 1979).

Page 28. "If I Stand" by Rich Mullins and Steve Cudworth, © 1988 Edward Grant, Inc. (ASCAP), *Winds of Heaven, Stuff of Earth* (Nashville: Reunion, 1988).

Page 36. "Hallelujahs" by Chris Rice, © 1995 Clumsy Fly Music, Inc. (ASCAP), *Deep Enough to Dream* (Nashville: Rocketown, 1997).

Page 37. "How Great Thou Art!" by Stuart K. Hine, © 1953, 1955 Manna Music, Inc. All rights reserved. *Praise!* (Grand Rapids, Michigan: Zondervan, 1979).

Page 41. "GOD" by Rebecca St. James and Tedd T., © 1996 Up In The Mix Music (BMI) and Babbitsong Music (BMI), *GOD* (Nashville: Forefront, 1996).

Page 48. "Joyful, Joyful, We Adore Thee" by Henry Van Dyke, *Praise!* (Grand Rapids, Michigan: Zondervan, 1979).

Page 49. "Hard To Get" by Rich Mullins © 1998 Liturgy Legacy Music (ASCAP), *The Jesus Record* (Nashville: Word, 1998).

Page 60. "The Maker of Noses" by Rich Mullins and Beaker, © 1992 BMG Songs, Inc. (ASCAP), *The World As Best As I Remember It, Volume Two* (Nashville: Reunion 1992).

Page 61. "Chorus of Faith" by Michael Card and Phil Naish, © 1994 Birdwing Music / Devaub Music (BMG Songs, Inc.) (ASCAP), *Joy In The Journey: Ten Years of Greatest Hits* (Brentwood, Tennessee: Sparrow, 1994).

Page 68. "I See You" by Rich Mullins, © 1991 Edward Grant, Inc. (ASCAP), *The World As Best As I Remember It, Volume One* (Nashville: Reunion, 1991).

Pages 70–73. "All Creatures of Our God and King" by St. Francis of Assisi (translated by William H. Draper), *Praise!* (Grand Rapids, Michigan: Zondervan, 1979).

FOR MORE INFORMATION ABOUT POSTMODERNISM AND A CHRISTIAN RESPONSE TO IT, PLEASE READ THE FOLLOWING BOOKS:

Groothius, Douglas R. *Truth Decay: Defending Christianity Against the Challenges of Postmodernism* (Downers Grove, IL: Intervarsity Press, 2000).

Petersen, Randy. *My Truth, Your Truth, Whose Truth?* (Wheaton, IL: Tyndale, 2000).

Veith, Gene Edward Jr. *Postmodern Times: A Christian Guide to Contemporary Thought and Culture* (Wheaton, IL: Crossway Books, 1994).

To order additional copies of

humble feelings

Have your credit card ready and call

Toll free: (877) 421-READ (7323)

or send $23.99* each plus $4.95 S&H** to

WinePress Publishing
PO Box 428
Enumclaw, WA 98022

www.winepresspub.com

*WA residents, add 8.4% sales tax

**add $1.00 S&H for each additional book ordered